HOW BLESSED DO YOU WANT TO BE?

MAKE THE CHOICE
THAT MAKES THE DIFFERENCE

by

Mylon Le Fevre

Harrison House
Tulsa, Oklahoma

Unless otherwise indicated, all Scripture quotations are taken from the *King James Version* of the Bible.

Scripture quotations marked (AMP) are taken from *The Amplified® Bible, Old Testament,* copyright © 1965, 1987 by The Zondervan Corporation. *The Amplified Bible, New Testament,* copyright © 1954, 1958, 1987 by The Lockman Foundation. Used by permission.

Scripture quotations marked (NIV) are taken from the *Holy Bible, New International Version®*. NIV®. Copyright © 1973, 1978, 1984 by International Bible Society. Used by permission of Zondervan Publishing House. All rights reserved.

Scripture quotations marked (NASB) are taken from the *New American Standard Bible®*. Copyright © 1960, 1962, 1963, 1968, 1971, 1972, 1973, 1975, 1977 by The Lockman Foundation. Used by permission.

Scripture quotations marked (NKJV) are taken from the *New King James Version*. Copyright © 1982 by Thomas Nelson, Inc. Used by permission. All rights reserved.

Definitions of Greek and Hebrew words are taken from *The Exhaustive Concordance of the Bible* by James Strong, Hendrickson Publishers.

All direct quotes from The Holy Bible are italicized with the author's emphasis in boldfaced type.

07 06 05 04 03   10 9 8 7 6 5 4 3 2 1

How Blessed Do You Want To Be?—
Make the Choice That Makes the Difference
ISBN 1-57794-551-4
Copyright © 2003 by Mylon Le Fevre
P.O. Box 822148
Fort Worth, TX 76182-2148

Published by Harrison House, Inc.
P.O. Box 35035
Tulsa, OK 74153

INTRODUCTION

Real Christianity is very simple. Here's the deal (God calls it the covenant) that He wants to make with you through His Son, Jesus Christ.

Jesus says, "You give Me your life and I'll give you Mine. You give Me your love, respect, reverence, honor, and obedience. Put Me first. Trust Me with your hopes, dreams, relationships, career, and finances. In return I'll give you My anointing, which includes: wisdom, favor, supernatural love, joy, peace, divine health, strength, grace, mercy, insight, discernment, and the power to create wealth—so much so that all people will call you blessed!"

Isaiah 61:9 (AMP): *"...All who see them [in their prosperity] will recognize and acknowledge that they are the people whom the Lord has blessed."*

CONTENTS

Foreword

by Kenneth Copeland

Dear Reader,

You will see in Chapter One that Mylon was, because of the lack of wisdom and understanding, living in fear and financial bondage. That's the condition he was in when Gloria and I first met him. He was also having some serious problems physically, especially with his heart. However, Mylon was also one of the hungriest men for God I had ever met. The Lord Jesus instructed us to throw out the meat and he hit it like a tiger. He went after the Word of faith with a vengeance. Night and day he listened to tapes, read, and absorbed all he could get his hands on. Since then, he has never let up. Not even after he was completely healed. He still has that heart hunger to more intimately know Jesus.

Gloria and I have had the privilege of watching Mylon and his ministry grow into a mighty force of deliverance. So we know first hand that he knows what he's talking about. "How Blessed Do You Want To Be?" is more than just a good book. It's a carry-with-you handbook on receiving from God. It is full of Scriptures that will fill your heart and mouth with the faith of God. Read it, then read it again. Then go to your Bible and study all the Scripture references. I can promise you you'll be glad you did. It works! Always! The Word of the Living God has done the very same things for Gloria and me as it has for Mylon and Christi. It will do the same for you.

Jesus is Lord,
Kenneth Copeland

Dedication

First and foremost, I dedicate this book to Holy God, the Father of my Lord Jesus Christ.

To my precious wife Christi, my magnificently good and perfect gift from God.

To my awesomely wonderful and godly daughter Summer and son-in-law Peter Furler, whose anointed ministry, the contemporary Christian band "Newsboys," is changing the lives of hundreds of thousands of young people for Jesus.

To my Mom, Eva Mae Le Fevre, who never stopped praying for me and taught me to sing about Jesus.

To my father and mother in the faith, Kenneth and Gloria Copeland, who lovingly taught me how to prosper and live peacefully, fearlessly, and joyfully by faith.

To Kenneth E. and Oretha Hagin, Pastors Kenneth and Lynette Hagin, and Craig and

Missy Hagin for helping Christi and me to enter into this new phase of our ministry.

To all my other heroes of faith who have set the example of integrity in ministry. May the blessings of God overtake you today!

1

Prosperity Is God's Idea

The Word of God has so much to say about God's great plan to prosper you. It has been my heart's desire to write this book for a long time because the truths that I want to share with you will change your life forever. They did mine! I want to help you prosper in a way that I know is real because I have lived it. Since the Lord first instructed me to talk to the partners of my ministry about their inheritance as children of the Living God, my own life has prospered in many ways, confirming in my heart that God's promises are good news!

I studied these Scriptures and listened to faith filled ministers teach the Word of God for years before I learned how to release these truths into my life. When I started doing the things

I'm sharing with you, I was deep in debt, poverty, and lack, even though I had generated millions of dollars in gross income from my career as a rock-and-roll musician. The money

that I made through rock-and-roll I wasted on drugs. When you're a heroin addict, you make very bad business decisions. So I wasted that fortune. I had material things without true prosperity because I was experiencing deep depression and oppression at the time. Without the Lord, there was always rebellion, pride, division, strife, and the power of disagreement with the people in my life and with God's divine plan for me.

After being born again I had one of the most successful Christian rock bands in the world and generated many more millions of dollars through the kingdom of God, and yet I was personally living in fear and lack. When I became a

Christian, my lack of wisdom and understanding left me believing that to be truly humble I could never be really blessed. My band, Mylon and Broken Heart, worked hard and eventually got out of poverty, but we never got out of lack. Lack means no matter how much money you make it is never enough to cover your needs and expenses. Therefore, you live under constant stress. Because of my ignorance of God's Word, I was not

I had material things without true prosperity.

sowing into the kingdom of God with purpose and direction from Him. Since then, God has revealed to me how to live in covenant with Him.

Since I started on this journey, He has proven Himself to me to the point where I can now say that I owe no man anything but love. I can go anywhere God tells me to go and do anything He tells me to do. I am free indeed! I am the head and not the tail, highly favored with God and man. I am healthy, free from fear, and blessed to be a blessing! *Now that is real prosperity!*

GOD WANTS YOU TO HAVE HIS BEST

God has more blessings for you than you have needs. In John 10:10 AMP, Jesus states the purpose of His coming to the earth. He says, *"I came that they may have and enjoy life, and have it in abundance (to the full, till it over-flows)."* Jesus came to give you abundant life. Abundance means more than enough, or too much. Please let me be real straight and down to earth with you. If you are not abundantly blessed and enjoying living for Jesus, then "you just ain't doin' it right!" Jesus wants you to have "too much" of the life of God. So much life that if you bump into someone at the grocery store, they experience His presence!

What would the life of God be like? Well, God doesn't have a headache today. He's certainly not having a stormy Monday. He doesn't have any credit card debt. In fact, where He is the streets are made of gold. He's not fighting oppression, depression, sadness, or grief. He's not worried about anything or having an anxiety attack. In His presence there is *"fullness of joy."* [1] God wants you to be full of joy!

God wants you to prosper by making the right decisions concerning His life. The most important decision you can make on your breakthrough to prosperous living is to choose to trust God. Many of us have confessed the following truth, "God is good all the time!" And I want to tell you that God is ready to prove it today! To trust God means you believe that He

> *The most important decision you can make on your breakthrough to prosperous living is to choose to trust God.*

is good and that He rewards those who diligently seek Him.[2] Trusting God means you believe He is totally honest, and therefore you are confident that His Word is the *truth*.

If you really trust God's Word, you will obey what He says to do. He promises to bless and prosper your obedience. There will always be conflicting choices to make, but if you choose God's best you will enjoy a wonderful life. Here are some of the things God's best and His life include:

- You can have a greater understanding of God's love for you.

- You can have peace in your relationships with others.

- You can have good health.

- You can enjoy consistent growth in your management of finances.

God intends for you to enjoy prosperity in all these areas of your life. In order to trust and obey Him you must believe that (1) He loves you, (2) He enjoys blessing you, and (3) He gave us His Word (the Bible) to help you be free, happy, and blessed. His Word (the Gospel) is Good News!

The Bible says,

> *"But without faith it is impossible to please and be satisfactory to Him. For* **whoever would come near to God must [necessarily] believe that God exits <u>and</u> that He is the rewarder of those who earnestly and diligently seek Him [out]."**

Hebrews 11:6 AMP

What that means to you is—you give God pleasure when you believe that He wants good things to happen to you! God loves to bless His children! Once that issue is settled then giving your life to Him is easy. Life becomes joy unspeakable and full of glory!

Too many people make decisions without God's guidance (His Word) and walk straight into discouragement and destruction, and consequently miss out on the abundant life that God designed for them to have. Many people believe that prosperity depends on having plenty of money. But I assure you that a billionaire dying alone from depression, cancer, or drug addition is not prosperous! Some pursue physical perfection to find happiness but discover that vain beauty cannot be trusted to bring lasting success. As a singer and musician, I have had many opportunities to see if fame and fortune generated true prosperity. Having some "celebrity" and most of the things that money could buy did not lead to the abundant life.

As I mentioned earlier, I have earned millions in my career but was left many times with nothing to show for it. I found that acquiring things does not lead to happiness, but *contentment* in a relationship with God will lead us to *all* things. Therefore, our relationship with Him should be our number one priority. Jesus said not to worry about your life, or food, or clothes. He said, *"...seek first his kingdom and his righteousness, and <u>all these things</u> will be given to you as well"* (Matthew 6:33 NIV). Praise God, I have experienced this truth.

PROSPERITY BEGINS IN YOUR SOUL!

Prosperity is a condition of the heart and is gained only through a renewed mind that focuses on an intimate relationship with God. Solomon, king over Israel and writer of several books of the Bible, devoted much of his writings to lessons on how to prosper. It is recorded that Solomon was (except for Jesus) the wisest, richest man in all the world, and that no man before or after him was wealthier or wiser than him.

Prosperity is a condition of the heart.

9

In the book of Proverbs, Solomon wrote down the truths that God taught him. We are wise to keep these truths in our minds as we make decisions:

*"Trust in the LORD with all your heart and lean not on your own understanding; in all your ways **acknowledge him, and he will make your paths straight**"* (Proverbs 3:5,6 NIV).

*"A greedy man stirs up dissension, but **he who trusts in the LORD will prosper**"* (Proverbs 28:25 NIV).

*"**A generous man will prosper;** he who refreshes others will himself be refreshed"* (Proverbs 11:25 NIV).

If we ask God for direction and trust in His instruction by obeying Him, God assures us over and over again throughout His Word that we will prosper. The Lord will prosper a generous man, but He also says, *"**He who conceals his sins does not prosper,** but whoever confesses and*

renounces them finds mercy" (Proverbs 28:13
NIV). This tells us that God is good and quick to
forgive, but if we keep going our own way and
don't obey His Word then we are running from
both God and His prosperity.

The Bible is the world's greatest record that
God wants to prosper you. He said, *"This day
I call heaven and earth as witnesses against you
that **I have set before you life and death, blessings
and curses. Now choose life,** so that you and your
children may live and that you may love the LORD
your God, listen to his voice, and hold fast to him.
For the LORD is your life..."* (Deuteronomy
30:19,20 NIV).

<u>**God has given you the choice**</u> between life
and death, and between blessing and curses; but
He also commanded you to choose "life and
blessings." **So prosperity and the abundant life
are yours simply by choosing God's best for
you.** On the other hand, there is no middle
ground. If you don't choose life and blessings,

then you have chosen death and curses by default. For example, if you do not choose a modem setting for your computer, your computer will choose a default setting for you. If you don't make Jesus the Lord of your life, Satan will lord over you by default!

GOD'S WORD IS HIS WISDOM

Prosperity begins with finding wisdom and understanding. God's Word says,

> *"Happy (blessed, fortunate, enviable) is the man who finds skillful and godly Wisdom, and the man who gets understanding [drawing it forth from God's Word and life's experiences],*
>
> *"For the gaining of it is better than the gaining of silver, and the profit of it better than fine gold.*
>
> *"Skillful and godly Wisdom is more precious than rubies; and nothing you can wish for is to be compared to her.*

*"Length of days is in her right hand,
and in her left hand are <u>riches</u> and <u>honor</u>."*

Proverbs 3:13-16 AMP

It's real simple—God's Word says that wisdom and wealth walk hand in hand. However much effort you put into studying and obeying the Word of God will determine the amount of riches and honor He can trust you with. If you truly believe that wisdom is better than silver and gold, then ask God for wisdom and develop the mind of Christ until you think like Him.

Wisdom and wealth walk hand in hand.

WHAT WILL YOU CHOOSE?

I made many choices that led me away from God's best. But there was a turning point in my life when my desire to intimately know God became first and foremost in my heart. John 1:14 says that Jesus is the Word. Therefore, to know Him intimately we must know His Word. I found that by studying God's Word I could literally put wisdom in my own heart and mind. That wisdom caused me to prosper. As I grew in the wisdom of the Word of God, it amazed me to see that my relationships with others prospered; my finances prospered; and even my health was restored to me, in spite of the abuse I had inflicted upon myself before I received Jesus as my Lord.

We begin to prosper in all areas of our lives when we call upon God to save us from our self-destructive ways. In response to our call for His help, God begins to reveal His Son, Jesus Christ, to us. As our thoughts realign themselves with the way Jesus thinks about the pursuit of happiness, we find that we are prospering on our journey through life. Jesus said, *"I am the way, the truth, and the life."* [3] This new way of thinking godly and truthful thoughts releases His prosperity to us.

Prosperity is not a selfish position. <u>It's God's Idea!</u> When you prosper from trusting in the Lord, it shows the world what a good God you serve. He gets the glory for the good things in your life when you openly trust Him, and others are drawn to Him because they see how good He is to you. He wants you to enjoy living for Him! *"O taste and see that the LORD is good; How blessed is the man who takes refuge in Him!"* (Psalm 34:8 NASB).

2

Jesus Is the Way
to God's Best

The blessings of God first began when I called on Jesus to forgive me for my sins and asked Him to show me His plan for my life. In an instant He gave me a new heart that was turned toward the desire to do what was right. I suddenly wanted to give to the world more than I was taking out of it. I am truly a witness to God's power to prosper His children. God adopted me into His family when I acknowledged the sin of wanting to go my own stubborn, selfish, lazy way. When I asked God to forgive me and received the sacrifice of Jesus Christ, He made me an heir to all that was given to Jesus. That same inheritance is available to all who call upon the name of the Lord.

Confessing that you need forgiveness and inviting Christ into your life is the first step in receiving God's best for your life. If you have never before put your trust in God to lead you in the ways you should go, I encourage you to do so right now. God is eager to hear from you. He wants to speak to you and listen to your concerns and lead you in the way that will benefit you.

Many people think they must *do* something to earn, deserve, or keep the provisions that God has granted to those who put their trust in Him.

We aren't saved by the things we do.

But the Bible clearly teaches that we are saved by grace through faith. (Ephesians 2:8.) We aren't saved by the things we *do* (not through our works); so none of us can boast of our own worthiness. And all we have to do to receive His grace is *believe* Him.

Grace is the greatest evidence of God's desire to prosper us. Grace is unmerited favor

18

and spiritual blessings to enable us to do what is right and to receive all the good things that we don't deserve. Grace is not earned—it is a gift from God.

The Bible says every person has sinned and fallen short of God's glory [goodness]. (Romans 3:23.) Not one of us *deserves* God's best. *"But God shows and clearly proves His [own] love for us by the fact that while we were still sinners, Christ (the Messiah, the Anointed One) died for us"* (Romans 5:8 AMP).

We deserved death for the punishment of our sin, but God's gift to us is eternal life through the union with Jesus Christ. (Romans 6:23.) Be encouraged by this great promise of God's love and provision for us.

"The Scripture says, No man who believes in Him [who adheres to, relies on,

*and trusts in Him] will [ever] be put to
shame or be disappointed.*

*"[No one] for there is no distinction
between Jew and Greek. The same Lord is
Lord over all [of us] and **He generously
bestows His riches upon all who call
upon Him [in faith].***

<u>*"For everyone who calls upon the*
name of Lord [invoking Him as Lord]
will be saved."</u>

Romans 10:11-13 AMP

The word "saved" includes all that we need
to live an abundant life. The original word used
in Scripture is the Greek word *sozo (sode'-zo).* Its
primary root is from the word meaning "safe"
and means to deliver or protect both literally
and figuratively. It is translated to heal, preserve,
save, do well, and be made whole.[1] So you could
read that verse like this: Everyone who calls
upon the name of the Lord, will be saved,
healed, preserved, and made whole—so that
nothing is missing or broken in their lives! All

this is available to those who recognize Jesus as Lord (Master, King) of their life.

Prosperity is the inheritance of Christ's righteousness in our lives. God generously bestows His riches on all those who call upon the Lord. This is the mystery of the Gospel of Christ, that while we were still sinning, Jesus died in our place so that we could be justified and brought into a right relationship with God.

> *Prosperity is the inheritance of Christ's righteousness in our lives.*

All we can *do* to receive the benefits of God's grace is to admit that Jesus, who never sinned, took our sin upon Himself so that we could stand blameless before God. Christ justified us by dying in our place in order to restore God's blessings to us. Then God raised Him from the dead so that we could have a risen, living Lord!

If you have never talked to God about giving Him your life, you can pray the prayer below, or simply talk to Him in your own words. He is not looking for ceremony or ritual, only for sincerity in your heart as you pray.

Father God,

I believe that Jesus is Your Son. I also believe that He died for my sins that have separated me from You. I believe that You raised Him from the dead, and therefore I accept Jesus as my Savior and Lord right now. I confess that I have sinned by doing what I wanted instead of trusting You. Please forgive me for ignoring You and Your Word.

Thank You for forgiving my sins through the sacrifice that Jesus made for me on the cross. Today I take responsibility for and repent of my sins. I turn to You. I give You my old, sinful habits in exchange for a pure heart that is hungry for You.

Fill my thoughts with the mind of Christ and send Your Holy Spirit to live in me. From this time forward, I will trust in You and Your Word. <u>From now on I will read Your Word and talk to You daily until I see Your face.</u>

Thank You for giving me the power to follow You all the days of my life.

In Jesus' Name, Amen.

No matter how you *feel* about it, if you sincerely prayed that prayer you will never be the same again! Now go tell somebody that you have accepted Jesus as your Lord. You have a new start in life and are an heir to the blessings of God!

ALL YOUR DEBTS ARE PAID

Once you put your trust in Christ, your life starts over under the new covenant, or under the new management, of God. Your destiny with death is replaced with the reward of eternal life.

The Bible refers to this as being "born again." You are no longer bound to old habits or patterns that lead to poverty, depression, hopelessness, or destruction.

You are now an heir to all the promises Jesus made in the New Testament and to the promises that God made to Abraham in the Old Testament. God's Word says, *"If you belong to Christ, then you are Abraham's seed, and **heirs according to the promise"** (Galatians 3:29 NIV).

Some covenant promises God made with Abraham and his descendants are in Deuteronomy 28:1-13 NIV (emphasis mine):

> *"**If you fully obey** the LORD your God and carefully follow all his commands I give you today, the LORD your God will set you high above all the nations on earth.*
>
> *"**All these blessings will come upon you** and accompany you **if you obey** the LORD your God:*

*"**You will be blessed** in the city and blessed in the country.*

"The fruit of your womb [your children] **will be blessed,** *and the crops of your land* [your career] *and the young of your livestock* [your investments]—*the calves of your herds and the lambs of your flocks.*

"Your basket and your kneading trough [your food] **will be blessed.**

*"**You will be blessed** when you come in and blessed when you go out* [your travel].

"The LORD *will grant that the enemies who rise up against you will be defeated before you. They will come at you from one direction but flee from you in seven.*

*"**The* LORD **will send a blessing** *on your barns* [bank accounts] *and on everything you put your hand to. The* LORD *your **God will bless you** in the **land he is giving you*** [He will give you land].

"The LORD will establish [publicly anoint] *you as his holy people, as he promised you on oath, **if you keep the commands** of the LORD your God and walk in his ways.*

"Then all the peoples on earth will see that you are called by the name of the LORD, and they will fear you.

*"**The LORD will grant you abundant prosperity**—in the fruit of your womb, the young of your livestock and the crops of your ground—in the land he swore to your forefathers to give you.*

*"**The LORD will open the heavens,** the storehouse of his bounty, to send rain on your land in season and **to bless all the work of your hands. You will lend to many** nations but will **borrow from none.***

*"The LORD will make you the head, not the tail. **If you pay attention to the commands of the LORD** your God that I give you this day **and carefully follow***

them, you will always be at the top, never at the bottom.

The bottom line of what these verses say is that God will grant you abundant prosperity in every area of your life if you will trust Him. Please remember that these covenant blessings were not Abraham's idea, they were God's. If you choose to enter covenant with God, which simply means you do things His way, then He will open the heavens to pour out blessings on you. He will bless the work of your hands so that you will lend to many and borrow from none. God will make you the head and not the tail. You will be what I call "slam dunk" blessed! (Blessed to the max!) Now that's prosperity!

God will grant you abundant prosperity in every area of your life if you will trust Him.

The Hebrew word translated "to prosper" includes all the positive attributes listed below:

Intelligence: God gives us a sound mind and anoints us with expert skills [wisdom] to follow His plan for our lives.

Understanding: He establishes us with supernatural understanding of what needs to be done in our personal and business affairs.

Security: We become secure, peaceful, confident, successful, and satisfied because we have learned to trust in and lean on God.

Advancement: We are no longer timid (fearful) because we know our faith in God is our shield and we are safe in His care. If He sends us on assignment we can break through our obstacles and go mightily towards the prize of His calling. We know that the work of our hands will be good, profitable, and blessed.

Righteousness: We have the right to come before God and ask Him for help. God will direct us in making right decisions that glorify His work in our lives.

✗ Success: Because we have His help we will be fulfilled and satisfied in our journey through life.

Many Christians do not know that they are heirs to this great inheritance of prosperity. As believers, we can expect intelligence to guide us, understanding to establish us, security to satisfy us, advancement to promote us, righteousness to clothe us, and success to follow us all the days of our new, born-again lives. What a great provision!

Once we invite Jesus into our lives, He takes our blame, shame, and rags upon Himself and covers us with His righteousness. He puts a new heart in us filled with His promises and loving ways. He sends His Holy Spirit to teach, comfort, and guide us in the way we should go. God recreates us to do good works that prosper us and those we serve.[2]

Think about it, the same Spirit that raised Christ from the dead comes to live in us.[3] He replaces all that is not of God with Himself. He doesn't do all the repair work in a day. But He does put the power within us to make the needed changes that will lead us to the good life.

The number one key to happiness is the renewing of our minds— learning to think like God.

I cannot overemphasize this issue: the number one key to happiness is the renewing of our minds—learning to think like God. *"And be not conformed to this world: but be ye transformed* (changed) *by the renewing of your mind, that ye may prove what is that good, and acceptable, and perfect, will of God"* (Romans 12:2 KJV). When you prosper financially you will have to be wise so you will know what to do with the increase that God brings into your life. If you really prosper, it will be the result of having biblical insight in the decisions concerning your finances. God's people should be better at whatever they do than those who live without

God, but **to be set apart from the world we
must learn to *think like God.***[4]

Proverbs 4:7 says that *"Wisdom is the princi-
pal* (most important) *thing"* and having the "mind
of Christ" is the foundation to our covenant with
Him! That's why it's important to keep God's
Word before your eyes. It is also why I am filling
this book with Scriptures that will establish your
faith in God's goodness. We must know what
God has to say about our life situations in order to
be wise in both personal and business decisions.

KEEP GOD'S WORD
BEFORE YOUR EYES

If you keep the Word of God before your
eyes, you will learn to think like God.[5] As a minister of the good news, I know that the key to
my own effectiveness is to keep God's Word
before me. I read it again and again, and even
though I've read it before, it speaks to me in a
new way each time.

I encourage people everywhere to spend time reading the Word of God and keep it in the center of their lives as they make decisions in their daily affairs. Before I was saved the devil stole many blessings from me because of my sins. But I lost even more because of my ignorance to the Bible! I did not know the truth (God's Word) and only the truth will set you free. Knowing God's will (His Word) for my life changed me and restored what I had lost by being apart from Him.

Reading God's Word will build your faith and keep you free from doubts and fears that would otherwise destroy your success. Teaching tapes are an excellent way to accomplish this. Christi and I are personally partnered with and support financially over 20 ministries who in turn send us their magazines, teaching tapes, books, and anointed music. This keeps us built up and strong in faith! Filling your mind with His Words will keep His thoughts in your heart and will lead you to all things that are good and perfect for you.

3

God's Guarantee

The Holy Spirit comes *into* us at the moment of salvation. *"And you also were included in Christ when you heard the word of truth, the gospel of your salvation. Having believed, you were marked in him with a seal, **the promised Holy Spirit, who is a deposit guaranteeing our inheritance** until the redemption of those who are God's possession—to the praise of his glory"* (Ephesians 1:13,14 NIV). The presence of the Holy Spirit in our lives is our guarantee to inherit the blessings of salvation.

As believers in Jesus Christ, the Holy Spirit dwells *in* us and He has promised to never leave us. But He also comes *upon* us to anoint us with power for the good works that will lead others to salvation and to the good life He has ordained for them. This place of anointing, His act of "coming upon" us, is an experience we should seek on a daily basis to empower us for godly living.

Be filled with the Holy Spirit on a daily basis by immersing yourself in the truth of God's Word. It is in this place of being filled and over-flowing that you will enjoy the prosperity of

 the abundant life. With knowledge of what God has said, you will be ready for any sur-prises the day may bring. Ask God to immerse you in His Spirit, love, and power each morning.

I pray for my family, my partners, and all those I minister to, that God would not only empower them with His Spirit, but also fill them to the point of overflowing. Matthew 3:11 says that Jesus will *"baptize you with the Holy Ghost, and with fire."*

BAPTIZED WITH POWER

When you are filled with the Holy Spirit to the point of overflowing, His power pours into the affairs of your day and affects the people you meet. You no longer have to face decisions with your limited understanding, because the Holy Spirit will give you wisdom, knowledge, understanding, and faith to choose God's best in every situation. The same anointing that was on Jesus can be in and upon you so that you can follow the Lord in obedience and in the ministry of sharing Him with others. Acts 10:38 says, *"How God anointed Jesus of Nazareth with the Holy Ghost and with power: who went about doing good, and healing all that were oppressed of the devil."* That is God's will for us! He wants to anoint us with His Spirit so that we can go around doing good and heal (deliver, release) all who are oppressed by (under the power of) the devil!

The same anointing that was on Jesus can be in and upon you.

Jesus told His disciples to wait for the Father's promise of the Holy Spirit, saying,

> *"For John baptized with water, but not many days from now you shall be baptized with (placed in, introduced into) the Holy Spirit.*
>
> *"...you shall receive power (ability, efficiency, and might) when the Holy Spirit has come upon you, and you shall be My witnesses in Jerusalem and all Judea and Samaria and to the ends (the very bounds) of the earth."*

Acts 1:5,8 AMP

We all need power, ability, efficiency, and might every day as we face new challenges. I'm writing this book because I want you to experience abundant joy, health, peace, strength, wisdom, and discernment that only the Lord can give you through being completely and constantly filled with His Spirit. And God wants it for you even more than I do.

Acts 19 records the testimony of some new believers. They had never even heard of the Holy Spirit. On hearing this, they were baptized in the name of the Lord Jesus. As Paul laid his hands on them, the Holy Spirit came upon them and they spoke in tongues (a heavenly language) and prophesied.

I believe that there are many people who struggle with their faith because they have not been baptized since they believed in Jesus. **Baptism is more than an outward sign of an inward decision. It is as a marriage ceremony between you and the Holy Spirit.**

Jesus is ready to baptize you with His Holy Spirit. He wants to anoint you with the fire of His power to demonstrate His goodness to a lost world. If you have not been water baptized or received the baptism of the Holy Spirit, speaking with a new prayer language, I encourage you to follow the Lord (become His disciple) in this next step towards your break-through to God's best.

First, find a faith-filled, Spirit-filled church where you can be baptized in water as a public testimony that you trust in Jesus alone for your salvation. Through baptism your body is immersed in water as a symbol of the dying of your old self. Jesus said, "If you confess Me before men, I will confess you before My Father and all his angels."[1]

Then ask the Lord to baptize you with His Spirit. Receive the gift of the Holy Spirit by faith just as you received salvation. I cannot overemphasize faith enough; *everything* you receive from God comes by faith (believing).

Through this simple act of submitting your whole self to the Lord, you will find that the Word of God will be clearer to you. Your under-standing of His unconditional love towards you will grow steadily through the days to come.

If you have been water baptized but have not experienced this gift of the Holy Spirit that is available to all believers, simply ask God for the release of your new prayer language. Say,

> *Lord, I want to be filled with Your presence. I want to be able to tell You and others how much I love You.*
>
> *Jesus, please give me the words to express my heart to the Father. Baptize me with Your Holy Spirit and anoint me to see and understand Your ways, Lord.*

Now by faith, like a child, simply begin to speak aloud whatever syllables come to your mind. At first it will seem so natural that you may think you are making up new sounds; but as the Holy Spirit gives you utterance and you continue on, you will find that new words come so quickly that it is difficult to keep up with all that your heart wants to pour out before God.

NOW STAY FILLED
TO OVERFLOWING
WITH THE HOLY SPIRIT

Many Christians testify of a time they experienced an in-filling of the Spirit of God, evidenced by a sense of great peace and power to overcome the obstacles to their joy. But sadly, many also admit that they never revisited that place of in-filling with Him.

Paul encouraged Christians in the book of Ephesians to be <u>ever</u> (constantly) filled with the Holy Spirit.[2] This refreshing is something that we initiate by taking time to seek God's presence in our lives. To be "ever filled" with the Holy Spirit means to go daily before the Lord with prayer and spiritual songs in order to fill ourselves up to overflowing with the presence of God.

> "Speak to one another with psalms, hymns and spiritual songs. Sing and make music in your heart to the Lord, always giving thanks to God the Father

*for everything, in the name of our Lord
Jesus Christ."*

Ephesians 5:19,20 NIV

Paul told the Corinthian believers that he
wished that everyone spoke in tongues during
their prayer time, for this is how individual
believers get "built up" in their spirit. First
Corinthians 14:4 AMP explains, *"He who speaks
in a [strange] (unknown) tongue edifies and
improves himself."*

ELIMINATE YOUR DOUBT

The more you pray in
tongues, the stronger you
become inside. As you continue you will begin to sense
that strength rising up in your
spirit. That is because you are

*When you
pray in
tongues you
are praying
out the
mysteries
of God.*

praying directly to God about secret truths and
hidden things that are not obvious to your

understanding. When you pray in tongues you are praying out the mysteries of God. First Corinthians 14:2 NIV says, *"For anyone who speaks in a tongue does not speak to men but to God. Indeed, no one understands him; he utters mysteries with his spirit."* We strengthen our inner man when we pray in the Spirit. Jude 20 NIV says, *"But you, dear friends, build yourselves up in your most holy faith and pray in the Holy Spirit."*

I love being in this secret place with God. Knowing the Holy Spirit is leading me to pray for things that are beyond my realm of knowledge gives me confidence and hope for a bright future. His only plan is to bless us. God says in Jeremiah 29:11, *"'For I know the plans I have for you,' declares the Lord, 'plans to prosper you and not to harm you, plans to give you hope and a future'"* (NIV).

God's Word says, *"You do not have, because you do not ask God"* (James 4:2 NIV). Through your new prayer language you circumvent your own doubt (you stop leaning on your own understanding) and you ask God to move on your behalf in areas that you may not have had the faith to request through your natural understanding. **This is a powerful step towards prosperous living!**

Read 1 Corinthians 14 if you have questions about the benefits of your prayer language. Can you imagine what would happen if all believers began practicing this daily in-filling of the Holy Spirit? As believers are "built up" spiritually, we will enjoy the prosperity of God's presence in our lives.

Look at the benefits of being filled with the Holy Spirit, as listed in Galatians 5:22-25 NIV:

> *"But the fruit of the Spirit is love, joy, peace, patience, kindness, goodness, faithfulness, gentleness and self-control. Against such things there is no law.*

> *"Those who belong to Christ Jesus have crucified the sinful nature with its passions and desires.*
>
> *"Since we live by the Spirit, let us keep in step with the Spirit."*

To be full of love, joy, peace, patience, and the other fruits of the Spirit is to truly begin to experience the prosperous place of God's best for you.[3] These gifts of the Spirit cannot be purchased with money; they were bought with the blood of Jesus on your behalf. **We can't earn the fruit of the Spirit through good behavior; but good behavior is the fruit of submitting to the Holy Spirit.** All we do is say "Yes!" to the Lord, and He fills us with gifts that bring prosperity into our lives.

Every morning my wife and I pray together for our family, our partners, and the decisions that we have to make for our ministry. We ask the Lord to clearly direct us in these decisions concerning our partners, itinerary, expenses, etc.

We always pray in the Spirit as well as in our understanding. Paul, inspired by the Holy Ghost, said in 1 Corinthians 14:15, *"I will pray with the spirit, and I will pray with the understanding also."* We also pray for the interpretation of the utterances (the knowing and the understanding) that the Holy Spirit gives us. Sometimes the Holy Spirit will immediately give me the understanding concerning the utterance that He has just given me or Christi. On the other hand, it may be a month or two later when we wake up one day and all of a sudden it is so obvious what to do about something that we didn't have a clue about the day before. He just gives you "the knowing" (revelation, interpretation) of His will!

Prayer keeps us focused on listening for God's Word for today. We know it is easy to get caught up in the activities of the ministry and completely

Prayer keeps us focused on listening for God's Word for today.

miss the unexpected turn that the Lord would have wanted us to take. God promises to give wisdom to anyone who asks Him for guidance. James 1:5 says, *"If any of you lacks wisdom, he should ask God, who gives generously to all without finding fault, and it will be given to him"* (NIV).

God is full of new and fresh ideas that He wants to impart to us. He speaks through His written Word and His spoken Word to give us power, ability, efficiency, and might every day as we face new challenges. What He blessed last week may not be what He wants to do this week. So we seek His Word daily and believe for His Spirit to fill us, direct us, and build us up for tomorrow.

4

God's Best Is More
Than Enough

I encourage you to *enlarge your vision and your expectation of God's provision!* Every believer has been called by the Lord to go and make disciples of all nations, baptizing them in the name of the Father, the Son, and the Holy Spirit, and teaching them to obey everything God's Word has commanded us. He promises to be with us even to the very end of the age.[1]

Bible prophecy and current events confirm that Jesus is coming soon! Reaching the world with the gospel is a corporate task of the body of Christ that requires prosperity in our individual lives. Some of us go into all the world to make disciples and some of us supply the needs of those who go. This task will require energy from healthy bodies, healthy finances, and healthy relationships with each other. These are fruits of prosperous living. The good news is that God promised to equip us with all that we need to fulfill this great commission.

Money is not the sole expression of prosperity.

I hope that you can see that money is not the sole expression of prosperity. On the other hand, it is imperative that you realize that wealth is an important part of the provision of God's blessing. He wants our wealth to glorify Him, but He does not want the love of money (the root of all evil) to seduce us to satisfy our lusts.

God promises, *"A good man leaves an inheritance for his children's children, but a sinner's wealth is stored up for the righteous"* (Proverbs 13:22 NIV). In these last days before the return of the Lord, we can expect that increase of wealth to God's people so that His covenant can be established in the earth.

An example of God's ability to suddenly provide wealth to His children is found in 2 Kings 6 and 7.

Mylon and Broken Heart

God's enemies abandoned their siege against Israel, fleeing in sudden confusion and leaving behind their food, clothing, gold, and silver for the starving people of Israel.

BE A BLESSING

In Genesis 12:3, God said to Abraham, *"I will bless those who bless you, and whoever curses you I will curse; and **all peoples on earth will be blessed through you"*** (NIV). God is outlining the purpose of His blessing to Abraham. **We are blessed so that we can be a blessing to others.**

We are heirs to the promises that God made to Abraham, and this Scripture shows that

God's blessings are more than enough so that we will have an abundance with which to bless others. In fact, all peoples on the earth are to be blessed through us. I've read that statisticians claim that there are more people on the earth today than the combined number who have ever lived since the beginning of time. In order for all these people to be blessed through us (the church), we need to be *very, very blessed!*

God will establish His covenant of blessing at our houses to draw all men unto Himself. Deuteronomy 8:18 AMP (emphasis mine) says, ***"But you shall [earnestly] remember the Lord your God, for it is <u>He</u> Who <u>gives you power to get wealth</u>, that <u>He may establish His covenant which He swore to your fathers</u>*** (Abraham), ***as it is this day."***

God gives us the power to get wealth so that He may prove His goodness and integrity to us! Abraham was willing to act on God's Word in faith that God's promises were true. He even trusted God when God asked him to give up his only son, Isaac, whom he loved more than his own life. (Read about the test of Abraham's faith in Genesis 22.) This test of faith was a forerunner to help us understand what God did for us when He gave His Son, Jesus, to die in our place. Abraham trusted God's promise of provision even when he didn't understand God's request.

Abraham trusted God's promise of provision even when he didn't understand God's request.

We qualify for Abraham's blessings the same way he did—by believing in the goodness of God and His promises. In fact, our inheritance through Jesus Christ is even better than all that is promised to us through His old covenant with Abraham.[2] Abraham's covenant was conditional on man's ability to obey the law—Jesus obeyed the law on our behalf. We now have rights to the covenant blessings through our faith in Christ's provision rather than through our own ability. Hallelujah! This doesn't mean that we don't need to obey God's Word, but it does mean that we have His grace and mercy just in case we miss it!

While Abraham and his early descendants had to struggle with their old nature in order to obey the commands of God, Jesus gave us the power to obey God's commands by placing His own Spirit within us. His Holy Spirit changes the very desire of our hearts and causes us to want to obey God willingly and cheerfully.[3]

PROSPERITY IS GOD'S PROMISE

Believe God for prosperity in every area of your life! The purpose of prospering in our health, in our minds, and in our finances is so that we will have more than enough to establish evidence of God's covenant on this earth today!

According to the book of Romans, faith comes when we *hear* God's Word.[4] Praying out loud and confessing His Word are powerful ways that God has shown us to renew our minds to His supernatural plan and purpose. When we are in agreement with God, our prayers become powerful and we see His Word happen in our lives!

You should daily read His Word and then frequently proclaim (or confess) it over your own life until you see its fruit. Below are some of the scriptural confessions that I speak over my family, my staff, my partners, and myself. I actually pray these words out loud so that I hear these biblical concepts resounding through my heart and mind.

Remember, faith comes by hearing—and hearing by the Word of God. I learned some of these confessions from a book by Charles Capps called *God's Creative Power*.[5] I encourage you to look up these Scriptures and then confess these paraphrased and personalized truths from God's Word into your own life:

I delight myself in the Lord and He gives me the desires of my heart. (Psalm 37:4.)

Christ has redeemed me from the curse of the law. (Galatians 3:13.)

Christ has redeemed me from poverty, sickness, and spiritual death. (Deuteronomy 28.)

I have given and it is given unto me good measure, pressed down, shaken together, running over; men give unto my bosom. (Luke 6:38.)

With what measure I measure, it is measured unto me. I sow bountifully; therefore, I reap bountifully. I give cheerfully and My God has made all grace abound toward me. Having all sufficiency of all things I do abound to all good works. (2 Corinthians 9:6-8.)

I have no lack for my God supplies all of my needs according to His riches in glory by Christ Jesus. (Philippians 4:19.)

The Lord is my Shepherd and therefore I do not want or lack. (Psalm 23:1.)

For He came that I might have life and have it more abundantly. (John 10:10.)

I know the grace of my Lord Jesus Christ, that though He was rich, yet for my sake He became poor, so that I through His poverty might be rich. (2 Corinthians 8:9.)

All who see me in my prosperity will recognize and acknowledge that I am a person whom the Lord has blessed. (Isaiah 61:9.)

*Father, I thank You that **above all things** that You want me to prosper and be in health, even **as my soul prospers.*** (3 John 2.)

The Lord takes pleasure in the prosperity of His servants, and Abraham's blessings are mine. (Psalm 35:27.)

For poverty He has given me wealth, for sickness He has given me health, for death He has given me eternal life. (2 Corinthians 8:9.)

When we speak these biblical principles into our lives, we are not wasting time. Speaking God's Word is not a boring religious ceremony. Jesus is the High Priest of our confession (Hebrews 3:1), and when we believe and speak His will, He sends His angels forth to accomplish His Word in our lives. Psalm 103:20 KJV says, *"Bless the Lord, ye his **angels**, that excel in strength, **that do his commandments, hearkening unto the voice of his word.**"* Who gives the Word of God a voice in the earth and establishes His covenant? You and I do!

THE PURPOSE OF PROSPERITY

God's intent to bless you is bigger than you! He wants to give you more than enough so that you can help others to find His grace for their lives, too. Remember, God's commandment is to *love others as you love yourself.* You will have to prosper in the love of God in order to obey this command. God wants you so blessed that if He tells you to give a widow in need a new set of tires or send a missionary abroad, you can quickly obey because you have an abundance. God wants you to prosper to the point where the only question you have to ask Him concerning finances is, "Lord, I have more than I need or want, who do You want me to be a blessing to today?" This of course does not come overnight but is a guaranteed process. As you invest time and resources into the lives of others, God will multiply your seed back to you as evidence of His promise to you.

All believers are called to be ministers and witnesses to the world. The greatest blessing of ministry is to see people saved, healed, delivered, filled with the Holy Spirit, and prospering in the promises of God. **When you live so that others desire to serve God, you are truly prospering in the way that glorifies God.**

The purpose of prosperity is that we are blessed to be a blessing to others. God does not prosper us so that we can live in an ivory palace and sit around watching TV like a hound dog all day. We enjoy God in the supernatural realm and we manifest His presence through the natural realm. Remember <u>we Christians live by faith</u>, but <u>the world still lives</u> and makes all their decisions <u>by sight</u> (what they call common sense or their own understanding), which does not require faith.

The purpose of prosperity is that we are blessed to be a blessing to others.

In order to live by faith, the Word says that we cannot lean on our own understanding.[6] We choose the life of God, His Word, and His way by faith; then God's spiritual blessings pour into our lives and are visible in the natural realm. It is in this natural realm where others *see* His blessing on our finances, health, and relationships with both God and man. **It is very important to God that others see us blessed.** Again, Isaiah 61:9 AMP says, *"...All* *who see them [in their prosperity] will recognize and acknowledge that they are the people whom the Lord has blessed."*

People who don't know God need to see God's blessings on us in order to choose Him for their lives, too. His love makes us healthier, wealthier, wiser, and kinder. His presence makes us more peaceful, more lovable, more patient, slow to anger, quick to forgive, full of joy, and overflowing in love. In other words, as we are blessed by His love, it is inevitable that we will bless others and they will taste and see that the Lord is good!

DON'T HIDE GOD'S BLESSINGS

Some Christians hide the covenant blessings that God has given them because they have let unbelievers and people who don't trust God make them feel guilty for being blessed. I used to be ashamed of the good life God had blessed me with because I didn't know it was a part of

His covenant to be blessed. I've known pastors who did things God's way for twenty-five years and He really blessed them. But they were afraid that if people saw their blessings they would stop giving to the needs of the church or would think that they had lacked integrity in their management of the ministry. So they drove their old van to church and kept the new car God had given them at their second home, which was nicer than the parsonage, because they feared what the people would say. God said you can either please Him or man. But if you make decisions because of what others might think or say, you will never please God.[7] **If you make decisions in an effort to please everybody <u>else</u>, then you will not be free to please God!**

I believe it is a sin to hide the blessings of God. It is a response based on fear instead of faith. The act of hiding God's blessings shows that we are actually ashamed of the fact that God did what He said He would do. That attitude hides God's glory and His integrity from the people's eyes. If we don't let people see us in our prosperity, they will never see how good God is. So I am determined that I will not hide this evidence that <u>people who serve God with wisdom are blessed</u>! I do not want to hide the glory of God. God's Word works!

The act of hiding God's blessings shows that we are actually ashamed of the fact that God did what He said He would do.

We should not flaunt or be proud of our blessings, because they come from God. Only He deserves the glory for His goodness in our lives. Also, we must never imply that prosperity is godliness. Again, wisdom is the most important thing to God and supernatural increase comes only from Him.

God wants you to be a peaceful, generous, healthy, wealthy child of God. He wants everyone who reads this book to come to the place where they can do anything He tells them to do. For you to prosper in God is what my ministry is about. I would never preach a gospel that would only prosper ministers. If *The* Gospel doesn't prosper every believer then it is not Good News after all. <u>God's Word will prosper anyone who believes, speaks, and obeys it</u>!

5

Just Do It

God receives the glory when His children are walking in His promises. Jesus said, *"And **I will** do whatever you ask in my name, so that the Son may bring glory to the Father. You may **ask me for anything** in my name, and **I will do it**"* (John 14:13,14 NIV).

Many people are not prospering simply because they do not know how to receive God's best. Our first step of obedience to receive the above promise is to simply ask and believe God.

This book was not written to teach you to simply gain wealth, but to show you the way to a prosperous relationship with God. Obedience to God's Word is an important key to receiving God's best for your life. I love to obey God and

I've learned to act quickly when I clearly hear His voice. Obedience keeps my relationship with Him vibrant and fresh. I am enjoying serving God more today than ever in all the years I have walked with Him.

 God has blessed my marriage, ministry, and music beyond my greatest expectations. These last few years have been the best years of my life. I am refreshed, renewed, and filled with holy energy for the future! On the other hand, some of the harvest I am now reaping comes from seeds that were sown during seasons of storms.

A relevant story of the consequence of disobedience is found in the Old Testament. King Saul did not obey God's instruction because he was more attracted to wealth and power than to the Word of the Lord. As a result, he lost his fortune, his position, and his relationship with God. The account of his downfall is found in 1 Samuel 15 when God told Saul to destroy the evil reign of the Amalekites who were enemies to Israel. Saul was to kill the oxen, sheep, camels, and donkeys, but he spared king Agag and took the best of his livestock.

When the prophet Samuel confronted Saul about his disobedience, Saul defended himself by saying that he took the animals to sacrifice to God.

But Samuel replied: *"Does the LORD delight in burnt offerings and sacrifices as much as in obeying the voice of the LORD?* **To obey is better than sacrifice,** *and to heed is better than the fat of rams"* (v. 22 NIV).

Samuel told Saul that because he had rejected the word of the Lord, the Lord had also rejected him and had torn his kingdom from him to give to another who was better than him. God could see into Saul's heart where he hoarded a lust for riches. On this fateful day, *Saul mistook wealth for prosperity,* but he learned that <u>*true prosperity is to obey the word of the Lord*</u>!

The wealth that is given to us as a result of our relationship with God should never become our primary focus.

God admonishes believers to trust in Him alone for our pleasures in life, saying, *"Command those who are rich in this present world not to be arrogant nor to put their hope in wealth, which is so uncertain, but to put their hope in God, who richly provides us with everything for our enjoyment"* (1 Timothy 6:17 NIV). <u>God provides</u> us with *everything* <u>for our enjoyment</u>. Now that is good news! Yes, He is going to instruct us to give as a lifestyle and bless a lot of people, but He also wants us to have so much left over that we are exceedingly blessed. He really wants us to have fun serving Him! Yet, the wealth that is given to us as a result of our relationship with God should never become our primary focus. The Word teaches, *"The one who sows to please his sinful nature, from that nature will reap destruction; the one who sows to please the Spirit, from the Spirit will reap eternal life"* (Galatians 6:8 NIV).

DO WHAT LOVE WOULD DO

God's Word offers clear and simple instruction on how God wants us to live. The two great commandments are to love the Lord God with all our hearts and to love others as we love ourselves. In these two commandments all of God's laws are fulfilled. To prosper in life, we are to do what "love" would do.

If we love God and others the way He has commanded us, it won't be hard to obey Him and give from our resources to help those in need. To truly glorify God through our prosperous lives, we must give more than money; we must also give love, time, compassion, mercy, and forgiveness. Jesus taught this in the following passage:

> *"But I tell you who hear me:* **Love your enemies, do good to those who hate you, bless those who curse you, pray for those who mistreat you.**
>
> *"If someone strikes you on one cheek, turn to him the other also. If someone takes your cloak, do not stop him from taking your tunic.*
>
> *"Give to everyone who asks you, and if anyone takes what belongs to you, do not demand it back.*
>
> **"Do to others as you would have them do to you.**
>
> *"If you love those who love you, what credit is that to you? Even 'sinners' love those who love them.*
>
> *"And if you do good to those who are good to you, what credit is that to you? Even 'sinners' do that.*

"And if you lend to those from whom you expect repayment, what credit is that to you? Even 'sinners' lend to 'sinners,' expecting to be repaid in full.

*"But love your enemies, do good to them, and lend to them without expecting to get anything back. **Then your reward will be great, and you will be sons of the Most High,** because he is kind to the ungrateful and wicked.*

"Be merciful, just as your Father is merciful.

"Do not judge, and you will not be judged. Do not condemn, and you will not be condemned. Forgive, and you will be forgiven.

*"**Give, and it will be given to you.** A good measure, pressed down, shaken together and running over, will be poured into your lap. **For with the measure you use, it will be measured to you.**"*

Luke 6:27-38 NIV

WHATEVER YOU SOW
YOU WILL REAP

If we sow loving acts, we will reap love. If we sow mercy, we will reap mercy. If we sow grace, we reap grace. If we are patient with others, people will be more patient with us. If we refuse to judge others, praise God we will not be judged! That's the way God's economy operates—whatever you sow you will reap, pressed down, shaken together, and running over! This is being a doer of His Word. In turn our health, our relationships, and our ability to serve God with all our hearts and minds will be blessed.

THE PROSPERITY OF PEACE

Another precious blessing of obedience is the peace of God. According to Philippians 4:7, the peace of God is so awesome that it surpasses our understanding. The peace of God acts as a guard to our heart and mind. People who choose the life of God find this peace, which is a fruit of obedience. When you walk in obedience to God's Word, you will grow in the wisdom of God. According to the Word, one of the many blessings of godly wisdom is peace. *"But the **wisdom** that comes from heaven **is first of all pure; then peace-loving, considerate, submissive, full of mercy and good fruit, impartial and sincere. Peacemakers who sow in peace raise a harvest of righteousness"* (James 3:17,18 NIV). God's wisdom will lead you to the peaceful places that are ready for harvest so that your storehouse is full.

The peace of God is so awesome that it surpasses our understanding.

In a world filled with chaos and calamity, peace is a most desirable commodity. Many would trade their fortunes if money alone could purchase it. But the prosperity of peace is not for sale; it is a free gift available to those who trust and obey the Word of the Lord and who practice the presence of His Holy Spirit.

John 14:23-27 NIV explains:

"Jesus replied, 'If anyone loves me, he will obey my teaching. My Father will love him, and we will come to him and make our home with him.

"He who does not love me will not obey my teaching. These words you hear are not my own; they belong to the Father who sent me.

"All this I have spoken while still with you.

"But the Counselor, the Holy Spirit, whom the Father will send in my name, will teach you all things and will remind you of everything I have said to you.

"Peace I leave with you; my peace I give you. I do not give to you as the world gives. Do not let your hearts be troubled and do not be afraid.'"

If we are truly in love with Jesus, then we say "yes, Lord!" when He speaks. Our obedience enables us to rest in <u>all</u> of His blessings. Make the commitment to the Lord today to live a life of obedience to everything His Word commands us to do. Then just do it!

6

Be Blessed To Be a Blessing

There are two kinds of people in the world: "givers" and "takers."

- Takers are people who seek wealth but will not share it. They just never seem to get enough. A thief is someone whose personality and character is prone to take from others. Satan is a taker—a thief who comes to steal, kill, and destroy.[1]

- Givers are people who seek God and who <u>eventually</u> have more than enough. God is a giver, *"For <u>God so loved</u> the world that **He gave His only begotten son**"* (John 3:16). Giving is God's personality and His character.

Ephesians 5:1 says that we are to be imitators of Christ, who is the exact representation of God. Since God is a giver, it is important for us to make the decision to also be givers. Then we need to know and understand how to give cheerfully, wisely, and obediently. But before we look at tithes and offerings, let me point out that God said it is just as important for us to know when not to give. God's Word instructs us to <u>give as we have determined in our hearts prayerfully and thoughtfully</u> before the Lord. His Word says that **we should be determined to be givers like Him.**

God said it is just as important for us to know when not to give.

We should never give reluctantly or under compulsion! In other words, we should never let someone talk us into giving by hyping, pressuring, or making us feel guilty. <u>We should give cheerfully and freely</u> **as the Holy Spirit leads us** because of our love for God and others.

Unfortunately, many Christians have been manipulated and made to feel guilty when it comes to giving. We should give because we love God and others—not out of guilt but out of love! If a minister says, "We are debt free and we don't owe anybody anything but love. We are blessed and able to do everything God tells us to do." Then some

Mylon and Christi

people think, *Well, I'm not going to give to him; I'll wait until I hear a good hard luck story.* They have actually been conditioned to give under compulsion or to respond to someone who talks about how hard it is to serve God and how He never really supplies all their need according to His riches in glory by Christ Jesus. That's not the truth!

I have noticed that the only people who go to a minister and say, "You need to sell that fancy car or house and give it to the poor," are the ones who are not tithers and givers. I have never heard someone who cheerfully obeys God in their giving say something like that because they understand that <u>you can't out give God</u>. Praise God, it is not a sin to be wealthy when God blesses you!

You can't out give God.

Someone who is in love with God and does everything God's way is never mad or jealous when they see those same blessings on someone else. They should never find fault with the blessings God gives others in the body of Christ. Instead, people who grow up in the Lord are thrilled when God's Word is at work in the lives of others. They want everyone to prosper from God's truth. They understand that God wants us to be rich in every way so we can be generous to others. He even gives us the seed to sow when we make the decision to be obedient to God in our giving.

Please read the following passage carefully:

"Each man should give what he has decided in his heart (we are supposed to decide to give consistently) *to give, not reluctantly or under compulsion, for God loves a cheerful giver.*

"And God is able to make <u>all</u> grace abound to you, so that in <u>all</u> things at <u>all</u> times, having <u>all</u> that you need, you will abound in every good work.

"As it is written: 'He has scattered abroad his gifts to the poor; his righteous-ness endures forever.'

"Now he who supplies seed to the sower and bread for food will also supply and increase your store of seed and will enlarge the harvest of your righteousness.

"You will be made rich in every way so that you can be generous on every occasion, and through us your generosity will result in thanksgiving to God.

"This service that you perform is not only supplying the needs of God's people

but is also overflowing in many expressions of thanks to God.

*"Because of the service by which you have proved yourselves, **men will praise God for the obedience that accompanies your confession of the gospel of Christ,** and for your generosity in sharing with them and with everyone else.*

"And in their prayers for you their hearts will go out to you, because of the surpassing grace God has given you.

"Thanks be to God for His indescribable gift!"

2 Corinthians 9:7-15

Attitude is very important to God! Giving is a form of worship.[2] When you cheerfully obey the Holy Spirit in your giving, it proves that you trust God.[3] He said that because of your joyful giving you will "in <u>all</u> things and at <u>all</u> times" have your needs not just met, but abundantly met! Then you can be a blessing in every way to everyone, everywhere you go!

RECEIVING THE
ABUNDANT BLESSING

God clearly promises an *abundant* return to the cheerful giver. The only time God said to test Him is in the area of giving the tithe to Him. He said:

> *God clearly promises an* abundant *return to the cheerful giver.*

> *"**Bring** all the tithes **(the whole tenth of your income)** into the storehouse, that there may be food in My house, and prove Me now by it, says the Lord of hosts, if I will not open the windows of heaven for you and pour you out a blessing, that **there shall not be room enough to receive it.***
>
> *"And I will rebuke the devourer [insects and plagues] for your sakes and he shall not destroy the fruits of your ground, neither shall your vine drop its fruit before the time in the field, says the Lord of hosts.*

"And all nations shall call you happy and blessed; for you shall be a land of delight, says the Lord of hosts.

Malachi 3:10-12 AMP

God promises to return more to you than you can store up. Remember, Jesus teaches us in Luke 6:38 KJV that when you give, then *"it shall be given unto you; good measure, pressed down, and shaken together, and running over, shall men give into your bosom. For with the same measure that ye mete withal it shall be measured to you again."* For when you sow generously, you will also reap generously. Remember, you can never out give God! I once heard a great man of God say, "If you could out give Him, He wouldn't be God." I agree!

Jesus asked us to consider how the Father cares for the birds that neither sow nor reap, yet the Father feeds them. He asks, *"Are you not much more valuable than they?"* (Matthew 6:26 NIV).

We are different from the birds because we can sow, reap, and gather into barns, so how much more should we rest in God's abundance than the birds of the air. We just read in 2 Corinthians 9:10 that He will supply the seeds to sow and bread for food, increase our store of seed, and enlarge the harvest of our righteousness.

When I get a letter from someone asking me to pray that God will bless their finances, in essence they want God to trust them with more money. God always reminds me that if they are faithful to Him (trustworthy) in little things (what He has already trusted them with), **He will make them** stewards (**His managers**) **over much.** We don't need to pray and beg God to do what He promised to do. He is honest! In fact, we can't stop Him from doing what He promised. Instead of talking to Him all the time about doing His part, we really should concentrate on doing our part. Our part is in being faithful to obey <u>consistently</u> in the little things; things, which we may think, are no big deal.

> "...'Well done, good and faithful servant! You have been faithful with a few [little] things; I will put you in charge of many things. Come and share your master's happiness!'"
>
> Matthew 25:21 NIV

*For only 10 percent, **God becomes your business partner** and rebukes the devourer for your sake.*

God wants abundance to flow out of our warehouses to others. When we decide to give God a tenth of all our income, He can then trust us with abundance (more than we need). When we are faithful in tithing and sowing (our seed is any amount above 10 percent of our income), then He will give us supernatural increase. For only 10 percent, **God becomes your business partner** and rebukes the devourer for your sake. Now, that's a great deal!

Malachi 3:8-9 says if we rob God (if we do not trust and obey Him in the tithes and offerings) we put ourselves under a curse. *"In tithes and offerings. You are under a curse—the whole nation of you—because you are robbing Me"* (NIV). Christ purchased our freedom and *"redeemed us from the curse of the law"* (Galatians 3:10-13). Of course, in order to be redeemed from the curse of the law you have to receive Jesus as your Lord (Master, King). *"If you confess with your mouth, 'Jesus is Lord,' and believe in your heart that God raised him from the dead, you will be saved"* (Romans 10:9 NIV). Then we must walk in that redemption by being obedient to His Word. *But* if you don't trust Jesus and won't obey His Word (even though you may believe that He is the Son of God and the only Savior of the world), then Jesus is not truly your Lord!

ENTER GOD'S
FINANCIAL COVENANT

This is important to understand: if you refuse to trust and obey God concerning your tithe and offerings then you have not entered the financial covenant that destroys the yoke of poverty and lack! You may have accepted Jesus as your Savior, but you have not made Him *your* Lord until you *believe that He is good* and therefore trust Him enough to *submit to His commands.*

If you haven't become subject to His Lordship, you will never grow in God. You may prosper in the world without tithing—you can work three jobs, or maybe cheat your way to what *looks* prosperous. But if you want to prosper God's way, you have to trust Him with your obedience, and obedience is better than sacrifice.[4] The Scriptures concerning the tithe are amazing. God has so much to say about the blessings on your tithe that it is impossible to ignore this direction from Him if you have made Him Lord of your life.

I know it may sound severe, but **if you don't tithe you are not in this financial covenant with God and you are still going your own way in your search for prosperity.** In other words, **you know there is a God but you don't want Him to be your God because you don't like His commandments!** Now please don't get mad or offended at me! God loves you and so do I. In fact, I have prayed many times for you and everyone else that will ever read this book. God wants you blessed and I want you blessed, but only the truth will make you free! Malachi 3:10 promises if we trust Him and obey and bring the whole tenth of our income into His storehouse, then the Lord of Hosts will open the windows of heaven and pour you out a blessing so great that there shall not be room enough to receive it! I don't know about you, but that is where I am headed—greatly blessed to be a great blessing!

You can't get that kind of financial blessing (with peace and prosperity in other areas of your life) while ignoring the command to bring tithes and offerings. This is a book about prosperity in God, so if you want to prosper I must bring this truth to the surface where it can be examined and released into your life.

You are the only person that can make the decision to break the yoke of poverty off your life and turn it into God's blessing through your obedience! You could get Kenneth Copeland, Kenneth Hagin, Billy Graham, me, and the Pope to pray for you, but until you obey God and submit to His commandments our prayers cannot remove the spirit (yoke, bondage) of poverty and lack off of you. **Only your faith and obedience can cause you to be prosperous in every area of your life!**

I cannot overemphasize this truth. You *bring* (not give) the tithe—one-tenth of your income—because it already belongs to the Lord.

Otherwise you rob God! *"Will a man rob God? Yet ye have robbed me. But ye say, Wherein have we robbed thee? In tithes and offerings"* (Malachi 3:8 KJV). An offering to the Lord is what you give over and above your tithe. Some people argue that tithing was an Old Testament command, but Jesus told the Pharisees in the New Testament, *"Woe unto you, scribes and Pharisees, hypocrites! <u>for ye pay tithe</u> of mint and anise and cummin, and have omitted the weightier matters of the law, judgment, mercy, and faith: <u>these ought ye to have done</u>, and not to leave the other undone"* (Matthew 23:23 KJV). It's clear that Jesus is saying, **"Yes, you should tithe,** but you shouldn't leave the more important things (the matters of love, mercy, integrity, and living by faith) undone." Then in Hebrews 7:8, *"Here mortal <u>men receive tithes</u>, but there he* **(Jesus)**

You bring *(not give) the tithe— because it already belongs to the Lord.*

receives them, of whom it is witnessed that he lives" (NKJV).

You can't get anymore New Testament than that!

POSSESS A LIFE OF LIBERTY

I have a passion to see people set free from the bondage of depression, debt, stress, poverty, fear, worry, sickness, broken relationships, and poor health. Praise God! That's exactly the works of the devil Jesus came from heaven to destroy! *"...For this purpose the Son of God manifested, that* he might *destroy the works of the devil"* (1 John 3:8).

Every month, about 50 percent of all prayer requests sent to our ministry reflect concerns regarding our partners' finances. The second area of greatest concern revolves around family members and relationships, and the third most mentioned area of need concerns physical health. It was their plea for financial freedom that first prompted me to write this book.

I want people to prosper spiritually, physically, emotionally, mentally, relationally, and financially. The good news is that God wants it more than I do! We pray for our partners every day. But once a week we get together with our staff to agree in prayer for all who write, call, e-mail, or fax to our ministry because it is scriptural to believe for God's increase over their giving and ours. We usually spend a couple of hours together in prayer. We pray in the Spirit as well as in our understanding and agree for God's provision to prosper all that His people are called to do. We speak the same blessings over their seed that Jesus spoke over the loaves and fishes. That blessing caused such increase that it fed thousands of people until they had *"as much as they wanted"* (John 6:11 NIV). If all the testimonies, praise reports, and miracles resulting from people doing what you have just read were written in this book, it would be the biggest book in the world!

YOUR BREAKTHROUGH TIME IS NOW

I have heard the Lord clearly say it's time for His people to break through every barrier that keeps us from being blessed in Him. _Now is the time for your breakthrough_! God wants to give it to you!

- If you need a spiritual breakthrough (increase in power in the Holy Spirit, or increase in faith, which is your connection to His power), God wants to give it to you!

- If you need a physical breakthrough (healing, divine health), God wants to give it to you!

- Or a mental breakthrough (peace, freedom from worry and stress, healing from past memories, increase in wisdom, understanding), God wants to give it to you!

- Or a financial breakthrough (a return on your sowing and a harvesting of your seed), <u>God wants to give it to you</u>! <u>Now</u>!

- Or all of the above and more, <u>God has it for you NOW</u>!

Both King David (who God said was after His own heart) and Paul (whom God used to write much of the New Testament) used the term "I believe and therefore I speak." Your breakthrough will come as you believe, speak (prophesy what God's Word says you have a right to receive), and obey (faith without works is dead and has no life)! I tell you in the Name of Jesus— <u>God is good</u> and He wants to prove it! He wants all your family, friends, and neighbors to see His goodness demonstrated in your life. He loves you and wants you blessed more than you need or want to be blessed!

Your breakthrough will come as you believe, speak, and obey!

The question the Lord told me to ask you is, "How blessed do you want to be?" The answer is, **"You can be as blessed as you want to be!"**

As you face decisions concerning your relationship with God or with your family, friends, and career, <u>you can choose the good life and abundant blessings</u>. Again, Deuteronomy 30:19 (NIV) says, *"…this day…I have set before you life and death, blessings and curses. Now choose life, so that you and your children may live."* Take time today and every day to let the Lord refresh you. Enter His gates with thanksgiving and enter His courts with praise. Worship Him for the splendor of His majesty. Honor Him and bless Him for He is good! His loving-kindness and tender mercy endures to all generations! Sit in His Holy presence and be filled to overflowing with His joy and peace as you become as **blessed as you want to be!**

ENDNOTES

Chapter 1

[1] See Psalm 16:11 AMP.

[2] Hebrews 11:6.

[3] John 14:6.

Chapter 2

[1] See James E. Strong, "Greek Dictionary of the New Testament," in *The Exhaustive Concordance of the Bible,* p. 70, entry #4982 s.v. "saved," Romans 10:13.

[2] Ephesians 2:10 AMP.

[3] Romans 8:11 AMP.

[4] See Proverbs 19:20 AMP.

[5] Ephesians 4:23,24; Romans 12:2; Joshua 1:8; Deuteronomy 28:1.

Chapter 3

[1] Matthew 10:32; Luke 12:8.

[2] Ephesians 5:18.

[3] 3 John 2.

Chapter 4

[1] Matthew 28:19,20.

[2] Hebrews 8:6.

[3] 2 Corinthians 5:17 AMP.

[4] Romans 10:17.

[5] Charles Capps, *God's Creative Power Will Work For You* (Tulsa, OK: Harrison House Publishers, 1976), pp. 21-23.

[6] Proverbs 3:5.

[7] Galatians 1:10.

Chapter 6

[1] See John 10:10.

[2] See Philippians 4:18.

[3] See Malachi 3:10.

[4] See 1 Samuel 15:22.

ABOUT THE AUTHOR

Mylon Le Fevre was born into a gospel-singing family. When Mylon was 17 years old, his first song, "Without Him," was recorded by Elvis Presley. Over the next year 126 artists recorded Mylon's songs. At 19 he made his first solo album and has sold millions since then.

Since accepting Jesus as the Lord of his life in 1980, Mylon has released 12 CDs, traveled over a million miles, been honored with a Grammy Award and four Dove Awards, and sold another million records. His latest CDs focus more on worship and praise.

In the last few years God has called for tremendous change in Mylon's life and ministry. Mylon explains, "Up until a few years ago I was a Christian musician who preached a little, worshipped a little, and rocked a lot. I'm thankful for the anointing of God upon our lives during that season, and I know that we have been and are led by His Spirit. But I have become a preacher/teacher, and worshipping God has become my lifestyle.

"Over these last 23 years, we've seen over 250,000 people make a decision to make Jesus Christ Lord of their lives, praise God. We've seen the goodness of God at every turn, and this new season of ministry has become even more glorious than anything we've experienced in the past."

Mylon's desire to minister to the church and evangelize the world is more powerful than ever. "More than ever before we need to proclaim the Word of God and to emphasize to every nation His promise to perform it for whoever believes it.

"I will always write songs to and about my Lord. The splendor of His holiness constantly amazes me. I believe the music that God gives me is anointed and has an important place in my ministry. But I am compelled to share His Word. It is the best news on this planet! I believe that if we do things His way, with His attitude, He will take us from glory to glory and teach us how to 'dwell in the secret place of the most High God' (Psalm 91) where victory in Jesus is guaranteed!

"In the last few years we have ministered to millions on Christian TV and in hundreds of churches, revivals, and crusades. God has allowed us the privilege and honor of teaching His Word at Bible schools, worship seminars, motorcycle rallies, Nascar owner/driver chapel services, NFL and NBA chapel services, and Christi's ladies' meetings. We have also had missionary opportunities in the former Soviet Union, Australia, Canada, the Philippines, Cayman Islands, Mexico, and Hawaii. We also have a commitment to Mike Barber Ministries to minister with him in the prisons of our nation where we are seeing revival explode."

With overcoming faith and an increasing understanding of God's Word and its promises, Mylon is looking forward to the future. Jeremiah 29:11 (NIV) says, *"For I know the plans I have for you,' declares the LORD, 'plans to prosper you and not to harm you, plans to give you hope and a future.'"*

We believe our future is very bright and full of promise.

To contact the author write:

Mylon Le Fevre
P.O. Box 822148
Fort Worth, TX 76182

or call:
(817) 281-2700

or visit our webpage:
www.mylon.org

If this book has been a blessing to you
or if you would like to see more of the
Harrison House product line,
please visit us on our website at
www.harrisonhouse.com

HARRISON HOUSE
Tulsa, Oklahoma 74153

THE HARRISON HOUSE VISION

Proclaiming the truth and the power

Of the Gospel of Jesus Christ

With excellence;

Challenging Christians to

Live victoriously,

Grow spiritually,

Know God intimately.